DATE DUE			

PARROTS

UNUSUAL ANIMALS

Lynn M. Stone

The Rourke Corporation, Inc.
Vero Beach, Florida 32964

Edited by Sandra A. Robinson

PHOTO CREDITS
All photos © Lynn M. Stone.

ACKNOWLEDGMENTS
The author thanks the following for assistance in the preparation
of this book: The Bird's Nest, Geneva, IL; Sarasota Jungle Gardens,
Sarasota, FL.

Library of Congress Cataloging-in-Publication Data

Stone, Lynn M.
    Parrots / by Lynn M. Stone.
    p. cm. — (Unusual animals)
    Includes index.
    Summary: Presents information about the physical
characteristics, homes, and habits of various species of parrots.
    ISBN 0-86593-280-8
    1. Parrots—Juvenile literature. [1. Parrots.] I. Title.
II. Series: Stone, Lynn M. Unusual animals.
QL696.P7S76   1993
598'.71—dc20   93-7461
                                                            CIP
                                                             AC

TABLE OF CONTENTS

THE UNUSUAL PARROTS

Walk into a pet store and you might hear a cheery "Hello!" That greeting may come from a parrot instead of a person.

Parrots have a very unusual skill. They are nature's greatest **mimics** of human speech. They can copy, or mimic, what they hear.

Parrots have been a favorite with people for hundreds of years. They are admired for their brightly colored feathers, or **plumage,** as well as their "speech."

Colorful feathers and "human speech"
make parrots popular with people

HOW PARROTS LOOK

Some kinds, or **species,** of parrots may be tiny—just 3 inches long. The macaws, the biggest parrots, are over 3 feet long.

All parrots have short necks and large, rounded heads. Their bills are short, thick and sharply curved downward.

Many parrots wear feathers of brilliant green, yellow, red and blue. Some, like cockatoos, have crests or long feathers behind their necks.

A parrot's foot has two toes pointed forward and two pointed back.

*Macaws are the largest
of the parrot tribe*

WHERE PARROTS LIVE

Wild parrots live in North America, South America, Australia, Asia and Africa. They are most plentiful in South America and Australia.

Most parrots live in low, warm rain forests. The kea, however, lives in the snowy New Zealand Alps.

In North America, several species of parrots live in Mexico and on the islands of the Caribbean Sea.

Many species of parrots, because they live in out-of-the-way jungles, are almost unknown to scientists.

Most parrots live in tropical rain forests

WHAT PARROTS EAT

Most parrots eat fruit, seeds and nuts. They have nimble tongues and bills. They can neatly separate seeds from their tough coverings.

Some parrots eat the tiny grains of pollen and liquid **nectar** that flowers make. Pollen-eating parrots have brushlike tongues to collect the pollen grains.

Black cockatoos of Australia are among the parrots that mix insects into their diets.

Eating fruit is a piece of cake for parrots

A conure finds a pink shirt hard to resist

Budgies are the most popular pet parrots

KINDS OF PARROTS

Scientists separate the 330 species of parrots into several groups. Parrots are grouped by their different shapes, sizes, calls and habits. A few of the parrot groups are amazons, parakeets, conures, macaws, cockatoos, cockatiels and budgerigars, or budgies.

The little budgies are the most popular pet parrots. Macaws are also popular, but they are extremely expensive. Macaws cost from $1,500 to $10,000!

The dazzling hyacinth macaw costs $10,000 in pet shops

BABY PARROTS

Most species of parrots nest in holes in trees or earth banks. The nest itself is usually quite bare, although African lovebirds carry bits of material under their back feathers to the nest.

Parrots lay two to eight white eggs, depending upon the kind of parrot. Parrots sit on their eggs for 12 to 35 days. Larger species take longer to hatch—and grow up—than smaller parrots. Some young parrots leave the nest after three weeks. Others stay up to four months.

Baby parrots seem to begin life as "ugly ducklings"

PARROT HABITS

Most parrots are **social**—they like each other's company. They often feed and rest together. During courtship, a male parrot may offer its mate a strange valentine—food brought up from its stomach. Parrots have even done this for their owners!

Parrots are acrobats in the treetops. They can hang from one foot, and they can use their strong, grasping bills like an additional foot.

Parrots are social birds, as these cockatoos show

PARROT TALK

Wild parrots screech and shriek. Captive parrots do, too, but they also mimic human words. That does not mean that parrots can "talk," or that they are unusually intelligent birds. It does mean that they are masters at repeating what they hear.

That ability, along with their curiosity and interest in being with people, makes them seem almost human at times.

The African grey parrot is a very skillful mimic. However, the record human vocabulary may belong to a budgerigar—531 words!

Trained parrots can shift from shrieking to repeating human speech

PARROTS AND PEOPLE

The human love affair with parrots is ancient. Yet America's only wild parrots, the Carolina parakeets, disappeared in the early 1900s. Today, 28 species of parrots are **endangered**—in danger of disappearing—or becoming **extinct.**

In some cases, too many have been captured for sale as pets. However, parrots have a larger problem—their rain forest homes are being destroyed. Forests are cut down for their wood and to make room for farmland.

Glossary

endangered (en DANE jerd) — in danger of no longer existing; very rare

extinct (ex TINKT) — no longer existing

mimic (MIH mihk) — to copy the call, color or some other characteristic of another animal; the one that copies or repeats the characteristic

nectar (NEK ter) — a sweet liquid made by flowers

plumage (PLOO mihdj) — the feathers on a bird

social (SO shul) — spending time in the company of others of the same kind

species (SPEE sheez) — within a group of closely-related animals, such as macaws, one certain kind or type (*scarlet* macaw)

INDEX